With love

from

_____

to

_____

LITTLE☆STARS™

LIBRA

A parent's guide to the
little star of the family

JOHN ASTROP

with illustrations by the author

E L E M E N T
Shaftesbury, Dorset ● Rockport, Massachusetts
Brisbane, Queensland

© John Astrop 1994

Published in Great Britain in 1994 by
Element Books Ltd.
Longmead, Shaftesbury, Dorset

Published in the USA in 1994 by
Element, Inc.
42 Broadway, Rockport, MA 01966

Published in Australia in 1994 by
Element Books Ltd.
for Jacaranda Wiley Ltd.
33 Park Road, Milton, Brisbane, 4064

Printed and bound in Great Britain by
BPC Paulton Books Ltd.

British Library Cataloguing in Publication
data available

Library of Congress Cataloguing in publication
data available

ISBN 1-85230-543-6

Contents

THE TWELVE SIGNS

Everyone knows a little about the twelve sun signs. It's the easiest way to approach real astrology without going to the trouble of casting up a chart for the exact time of birth. You won't learn everything about a person with the sun sign but you'll know a lot more than if you just use observation and guesswork. The sun is in roughly the same sign and degree of the zodiac at the same time every year. It's a nice astronomical event that doesn't need calculating. So if you're born between

May 22 and June 21 you'll be pretty sure you're a Gemini; between June 22 and July 23 then you're a Cancer and so on. Many people say how can you divide the human race into twelve sections and are there only twelve different types. Well for a start most people make assessments and judgements on their fellow humans with far smaller groups than that. Rich and poor, educated and non-educated, town girl, country boy, etc. Even with these very simple pigeon holes we can combine to make 'Rich educated town boy' and 'poor non-educated country girl'. We try to get as much information as we can about the others that we make relationships with through life. Astrology as a way of describing and understanding others is unsurpassed. Take the traditional meaning of the twelve signs:

Aries - is self-assertive, brave, energetic and pioneering.

Taurus - is careful, possessive, values material things, is able to build and make things grow.

Gemini - is bright-minded, curious, communicative and versatile.

Cancer - is sensitive, family orientated, protective and caring.

Leo - is creative, dramatic, a leader, showy and generous.

Virgo - is organised, critical, perfectionist and practical.

Libra - is balanced, diplomatic, harmonious, sociable, and likes beautiful things.

Scorpio - is strong-willed, magnetic, powerful, extreme, determined and recuperative.

Sagittarius - is adventurous, philosophical, far-thinking, blunt, truth-seeking.

Capricorn - is cautious, responsible, patient, persistent and ambitious.

Aquarius - is rebellious, unorthodox, humanitarian, idealistic, a fighter of good causes.

Pisces - is sensitive, imaginative, caring, visionary and sacrificing.

If you can find anyone in your circle of friends and acquaintances who isn't described pretty neatly by one of the above it would be surprising. Put the twelve signs into different lives and occupations and you see how it works. A Taurean priest would be more likely to devote his life to looking after the physical and material needs of his church members, feeding the poor, setting up charities. A Virgoan bank robber would plan meticulously and never commit spontaneous crimes. A Leo teacher would make learning an entertainment and a pleasure for her pupils.

So with parents and children. A Capricorn child handles the business of growing up and learning in a very different way to a Libran child. A Scorpio parent manages the family quite differently to an Aquarian. The old boast, 'I'm very fair, I treat all my children the same', may not be the best way to help your little ones at all. Our individual drive is the key to making a success of life. The time when we need the most acceptance of the way we are is in childhood. As a parent it's good to know the ways in which our little ones are like us but we must never forget the ways in which they are different.

LITTLE LIBRA

Making friends is never a difficult thing for the harmony-loving Librans. Good relationships are their main concern in life and they come well equipped with all the best talents for the job. Little Libras are a delight. Could this be the perfect child? In the early days it will certainly look like it. They will be agreeable to almost any parental suggestion, will be well mannered, and do everything with a winning smile that would disarm even the hardest heart. At the earliest age, Libras are aware of the needs of their friends and family and will go out of their way to be a credit to their loving parents when adult friends call. Their big drive is diplomacy, seeing both sides of any situation and needing to be fair to everyone at all costs. As they grow older this talent be-  comes more highly developed, making them adept little school arbitrators and expert at cooling down the tempers of battling classmates. In fact little Librans are distinctly uncomfortable when family rows occur, no matter how trivial, and until they are able to step in and stop them, they will take even the mildest altercation deeply to heart. So where's the snag with this little wonder? Libra children typically have an infuriatingly difficult time making up their minds. Always conscious of

the alternative choices offered, they will swing backwards and forwards in a haze of indecision often ending in doing absolutely nothing

at all. It will not be a long time before you decide never to ask again whether little Libra would like to wear the red or the blue coat when you go out. The consternation on that little face as she runs over the whys and wherefores of ensemble matching will make you realise that 'Would you try and button up the red coat when you put it on' is a better option. The old Jewish joke of the Momma who bought her son two shirts and on seeing him proudly wearing one the next morning said, 'You don't like the other one?', has got to be a Libran Momma. Make no mistake, however; lurking under this apparently yielding Libran nature is a strong will and a need to get their own way. Little Libra, being a proficient diplomat, will usually get it, though you may not fully realise what's going on. When all else fails, the charm will be switched on and you'll find yourself doing what you said an emphatic 'no' to half an hour before. They are not loners and may often infuriate you with their inability to keep themselves amused. Although often this is inconvenient you should not see it as a deficiency on their part. The Libran role in life is a strongly social one and they will always feel deprived if they have no one to cooperate with. Librans are team people and that just doesn't work on your own. Your young Libran will thrive on lots of conversation, lots of company, and very few choices!

THE BABY

This is the babe that'll take the prizes at the local baby show. It's not that all little Librans are the prettiest babies you've ever seen (though plenty are!) but they always manage to give the warmest little smile, come up with the cutest little expression and all timed to such perfection that the other kids just never stand a chance. Just as

 the judge peers at your precious pet, the giggle and the gurgle and the big eyes get working and it's a winning combination! Librans wanna be loved and come into this world with a head start on the rest of us. They seem to exist for company, and family and friends in abundance are all that your new arrival will need to keep as happy as the day is long. Baby Librans share the

baby Taureans' love of comfort and pleasure. The ruling planet Venus demands that everything is just so: blankets not too itchy, bottle at just the right soothing temperature and plenty of attention. It's never too early to start conversations with baby Libra and you'll be surprised at the early attempts to imitate your sentences. Later on there are going to be long, long, discussions and warm friendly arguments with this sociable little being, so better get practising as soon as possible.

The First Three Years

You may find your little Libran rather slow to start feeding himself purely because of the closeness of having you around at this regular ritual. This is no great problem to surmount as long as you don't just go off and leave him to it. Stay around and keep it chatty and remember little Librans will do anything to please. Walking is usually a different matter and is mastered fairly quickly and confidently. From now on you'll be followed everywhere. As soon as little Libra is on the move pattering about the house with confidence she's ready for the tinies' group. Search out local clubs for Mums and toddlers and you'll put your small socialiser into her native element and take a little of the strain off your constantly demanded presence. You'll be surprised how often your little one gets asked to parties and you'll glow with pride when you discover that all the other

Mums see your progeny as a good influence on the more rowdy element. Librans have a great appreciation of beauty, colour and music and should be encouraged to enjoy creative pleasures as early as possible. Remembering the decision-making problems, don't present little Libra with a giant paintbox with a thousand colours, keep it down to three pots of colour at the most and you'll get results. Bedtime may become a ritual of story after story and then a couple of calls later just to make sure

you're still there. Although beginning to become quite independent when in the company of small friends, your little one will often need reassurance that you still love them.

THE KINDERGARTEN

Already well practised in the art of making friends your little one should be in seventh heaven at nursery school. Best friends will be collected; little Libra is not one for great gangs but quickly sorts out special chums. Watch out though for the days when a very special friend turns her attention to another friend, your little Libra will be inconsolable and require oceans of reassurances to get back on an even keel. Relationships are meaningful and intense even to a four year old. Unlike many other small children little Libra learns very quickly to share and, quite uncharacteristically for little ones of this age, will politely ask for

a turn with a particular toy. Surprisingly enough it works even with some of the grab and run mob. Disliking inharmonious situations, your small diplomat will endeavour to set wrongs to right amongst the other group members and for this reason will become a really useful contributor to the little community, as they later will to adult society.

School and Onwards

'Fitting in' is a great Libran knack in any group situation and school is made for this. Most young people learn quickly that being different or standing out in the crowd at school makes for unpopularity. There is no chance of this with such a sociable child. Usually appreciating the rewards that go with good achievement, your little Libran will be a good scholar but not so outstanding as to become aloof from the rest of the

class. It's almost as if they control their output of work in order to keep the balance, quite bright but not too clever-clever! For this reason you may see on the end-of-term reports a 'could do better' but if it loses them friends you'll have to forget it. Encourage your youngster's invitation of friends to come round and watch TV or play in the yard after school, even if it means having to go to the cash and carry in order to deal with the high toll on cookies and cola. This is little Libra's top priority and will keep all else running smoothly. The great consolation is that the friends are well chosen and will never be rowdy.

THE THREE DIFFERENT
TYPES OF LIBRA

THE DECANATES

Astrology traditionally divides each of the signs into three equal parts of ten degrees called the decanates. These give a slightly different quality to the sign depending on whether the child is born in the first, second or third ten days of the thirty-day period when one is in a sign. Each third is ruled by one of the three signs in the same element. Libra is an Air sign and the three Air signs are Libra, Aquarius and Gemini. The nature of Air signs is basically communicative so the following three types each has a different way of expressing their communicative drives.

First Decanate - September 24 to October 3

This is the part of Libra that is most typical of the sign qualities. Libra is the diplomat of the zodiac. People born in this section of the sign are ruled by the harmonious planet Venus, giving them a natural charm and easy-going manner that makes friends wherever they go. Their answer to all problems is balance all the issues and choose the fair and peaceable one. Even rebelling against an unjust situation they will still manage to make their case known and achieve success without a disruptive battle. The supreme example of this is Gandhi's non-aggressive but powerful movement of 'passive resistance' in regaining India for the Indians and proving the great strength in this sign's natural peaceful reaction to even the most overpowering of opponents. Behind the Libran need to come to a fair conclusion lies a strong will that won't be denied. Often the recipient of their gentle persuasion is not aware of having had to make a complete change of direction, the process being achieved so smoothly. Although comfort and luxury are always part of the needs of this sign, mental calmness and peace of mind are of equal importance and many choose to find greater harmony in a simpler way of life. Brigitte Bardot gave up the fake glitter of the movies for her love of animals.

Second Decanate - October 4 to October 13

This is the Rebelling Diplomat. Ruled by the planet Uranus and the sign of Aquarius we have Librans who are prepared to be much more outrageous in their approach to the diplomatic arts. They have fewer problems with forthright speaking and have a confidence that knows that whatever they say, the world will see them sympathetically. They identify with the motives, hopes and fears of the common man and can always be found somewhere where there is a good cause to be fought. Their working tools are words and they are powerful in using them to achieve their ambitions. John Lennon set a whole great following on the search for peace and harmony not caring how eccentric he seemed and was loved for it. Bob Geldof's blunt call to arms of the music business was a notable example of the Libra/Aquarian in action. To be able to convert the pleasurable art of music into a powerful weapon against famine and hunger was a typical successful Libran answer to a problem of gigantic proportions.

Third Decanate - October 14 to October 23

This is the Versatile Diplomat. Having the extra influence of the sign of Gemini and the planet

Mercury there is an eternally young quality about these characters. Quick-thinking, they are masters of the art of the fast witty back answer. Their lives are probably more varied, moving between different projects easily and in some cases having more than one occupation. They are able to tap in to popular taste to achieve their successes and have the ability to adapt to new circumstances in order to stay successful. Lillian Gish the actress, star of the silent films, lived to be a hundred and worked steadily in movies for seventy of those years. She took to writing in the latter part of her life. General Eisenhower changed his occupation as soldier for politics and the Presidency of America. In the UK, singer Cliff Richard, at fifty, has as great a following as he did when he was a teenage idol. His other activity is as an advocate for Christianity which he considers as important as his musical career.

OTHER LITTLE LIBRANS

Mums and Dads like you delighted in bringing up the following little diplomats. Yours will probably turn out to be even more famous!

First Decanate Libra

Mohandas Gandhi, George Gershwin, F. Scott Fitzgerald, T.S.Eliot, Groucho Marx, Truman Capote, Ed Sullivan, Gore Vidal, Christopher Reeve, Brigitte Bardot, Julie Andrews, Ellis Peters, Harold Pinter, Meatloaf, Michael Douglas, Jim Henson.

Second Decanate Libra

Charles I of France, Guiseppe Verdi, Jean Antoine Watteau, Le Corbusier, Juan Perón, Lillie Langtry, Buster Keaton, Eleanor Roosevelt, Luciano Pavarotti, Charlton Heston, Jackie Collins, John Lennon, Thelonious Monk, Bob Geldof, Paul Simon.

Third Decanate Libra

Franz Liszt, Sarah Bernhardt, Oscar Wilde, P.G. Wodehouse, Lillian Gish, General Dwight D. Eisenhower, Eugene O'Neill, Rita Hayworth, Katherine Mansfield, Arthur Miller, George C. Scott, Roger Moore, Sting, Cliff Richard.

And Now the

Parents

THE ARIES PARENT

The good news!

If you're a typical Aries parent you're affection-ate, quick acting, and a bit of an individualist. Libran children are sociable and charming, and constantly seek and love the company of others. Their biggest social asset, always being able to see the other person's point of view, has a negative side that can drive the spontaneous Aries parent stead-ily up the wall. Decisions! Decisions! They just can't make them. Little Libra has an excellent logi-cal mind that accepts nothing at face value without

looking at the alterna-
tives. Great for friendly
argument, social con-
versation and the
accumulation of broad
knowledge. But what to
have for breakfast be-
comes an interminable
inquiry, and which
dress to wear, a two
hour debate. The Aries
parent can help initially
by firmly limiting the

options. Later, a little Aries logic - that any decision is better than no decision – may be acceptable.
Don't rush though, unless you want to change your
amiable little chatterbox and devoted companion
into a sulky, argumentative opponent. However, on
balance, there's less rough than smooth with little
Libra. Just to keep the balance, Librans need to

recharge their batteries a lot more than an Aries, that is if Aries ever needs recharging. Your energy and enthusiasm are unlimited but you can make the mistake of thinking that little Libra is just a lazy good-for-nothing, flopped out on the sofa, in front of the TV when there are important things to be done. Have a heart, Librans use up a great deal of mental energy, rolling problems around in their quick deliberating minds and that needs a break just as much as you need a good rest after a physical workout.

...and now the bad news

There can be times when you'll blow your top out of sheer frustration just trying to get little Libran to do something on his own. The pair of you really are exact opposites in the zodiac. One concerned with self-expression and the individual approach, the other with relationships and teamwork. Little Libra's need for someone else around is not lack of independence but a rehearsal for his role in life as a vital member of the team. Aries can explode with temper one minute and forget it the next, unfortunately your little one will not be so resilient and can suffer greatly if the harmony of the home is even mildly disturbed. You have a great deal to learn from each other if you can see each other's roles as complimentary to your own.

THE TAURUS PARENT

The good news!

The friendly, harmonious Libran and the affectionate, steady-as-a-rock Taurean parent should be as close as two peas in a pod. Some relationships thrive on competitive tussles, slanging matches, and slammed doors. Not so this one. The Taurean parent will soon notice how easily Junior fits in with any family plans. There's nothing weak-willed about this bright-minded child though, just a genuine desire to make you feel good. And if you feel good, so does tiny Libra. They are never 'loners' and, left to their own devices, often become lazy, listless, with 'nothing to do'. But their real talent is expressed in teamwork and group activity where they can develop their exceptional gifts of diplomacy. The Taurean parent will find it easier than most to deal patiently with young Libra's indecisiveness. Junior's keen sense of justice can see so easily the pros and cons that coming down on one side or the other can take ages. Social life will be most important to little Libra and there's no one better than the generous Taurean parent to keep

open house to this youngster's little friends. Mum and Dad Taurus can be really obstinate on certain points of view and, although Librans like a good argument, at the point where things look like getting inharmonious they will give in. It is all too easy not to notice that this is happening, with little Libra saying yes to everything just to please you. Family peace and harmony is so important to them that they can easily lose their own identity, wants and needs in favour of a quiet life. Allow your little one to win sometimes just to keep the balance right.

...and now the bad news!

Clashes should be almost non-existent in this relationship. However, the sheer luxury-loving, easy-going natures of Taurus and Libra could deteriorate into such self-indulgent inertia that Junior's creative potential remains unexplored. Both of you are ruled by the luxury-loving planet

Venus and for this reason can get a little too hooked on the pleasures and enjoyment of good food and just lazing about. A great recipe for producing a couple of well-fed fat cats. Why not convert the Venusian talents into shared creative and artistic projects. Both of you have the talent, and the joy of actually bringing something new and original into being will outweigh the self-indulgent pleasures. Usually Taureans have a talent for music and if you could encourage little Libra to share your pleasure and make sweet music together it would be the most delightful way to develop your youngster's good sense of balance and harmony.

The Gemini Parent

The good news!

You two could be the unbeatable chatterboxes of the zodiac. Nobody else in the family will get a word in edgeways. The quick-thinking Gemini parent thrives on good communications and will encourage wholeheartedly little Libra's potential for self-expression. The sooner this youngster gets to the chattering stage the better Gemini likes it. Right from the cradle little Librans are easy-going, anxious-to-please charmers – that is, until you leave them on their own. 'People who need people' must have been written with these company-seekers in mind. In this need to always be with someone else lies the Libran strength, and the Gemini parent will delight in Junior's quick development of diplomacy, logic, and ability to see the other side. You will undoubtedly produce a constant flow of stimulating information and knowledge to keep the relationship friendly and informative. Although essentially a lover of harmony and peace, your little Libran will

often quite surprisingly argue really firmly against you. The Libran nature needs to explore alternative ideas and weigh the pros and cons of any situation, but above all the motive is to be fair to all possibilities. Your Gemini wit can get sharp and hurtfully sarcastic when taken aback by an argument and it would be wise to realise that little Libra is not trying to be clever and score points but only trying to find the truth. Armed with this knowledge you can help your little diplomat become expert in the art of debate without forcing her to give in for the sake of peace and quiet.

...and now the bad news!

There may be times when Gemini's broad, scattered schooling will be too much, and too fast, for this youngster's compulsion to weigh every pro and con. The Libran desire to come to the perfect conclusion can result in exasperating indecision when faced with too many Gemini options. Constant pressure to give quick answers will be met with ' anything to please', 'whatever you think best' negativity. Both Gemini and Libra are good 'mind' signs, Gemini's faster but Libra's more thorough. Cut down the alternatives when helping Junior decide and you'll encourage balanced judgement rather than weak-kneed 'giving in'. You're going to have great fun playing word games, sharing artistic pursuits (especially things to decorate and enhance the home), social trips, and continuous conversation.

THE CANCER PARENT

The good news!

You're a loving Mom or Dad and nothing in this world, even your own good sense, is going to stop you spoiling this babe. The little Libran is all that a Cancerian could dream of. The Libran child thrives best on shared activities, and the Cancer parent, a natural home-lover, will not leave this child to 'go it alone'. It is not that Librans cannot stand on their own two feet, but they develop best through teamwork. Because of their natural charm and desire to get on with others, they learn quickly to see the other person's point of view. The Cancerian parent is imaginative and sensitive enough to provide good stimulation for developing the intellectual powers of the young Libran. If really left to your own devices though, you're a bit of a homebird, not being too troubled if you stay in and just potter around the house. You will be well advised to make a few concessions to your sociable little Libran who needs plenty of visitors and plenty of short trips visiting others. Your little one will be

a popular invite for all the local birthday parties because all parties seem to run a little more smoothly with a small Libran peacemaker present. Your Cancerian home will have to become open house to the many

friends this child makes, providing the company in which the Libran diplomatic leadership potential grows. The ability to see all sides of a question is young Libra's biggest advantage and conversely the biggest problem. The Cancer parent's overwhelming desire to give of the best may produce too many options, making decisions for the small Libran impossible. With Libra the 'set meal' is preferable to the 'à la carte' menu, at least some of the time.

...and now the bad news!

Even in the best of relationships, and this could be one of them, things can go wrong. Almost the only problem between your two signs will be the Cancerian over-protectiveness working with the Libran desire for an easy and harmonious life. Libra's not going to say no if you do everything for him because he doesn't seem to be managing very well.

You're just going to have to bite your lip and say nothing while you wait an eternity for your little one to make up his mind and get into action. Please resist the impulse to say 'Here let me do it' every time because it's easier. You'll become a slave; and even if little Libra dislikes you stepping in prematurely every time he's just about to decide, he'll never say. Little Librans don't like to offend. Even the Crab can be tough to be kind.

THE LEO PARENT

The good news!

Libra children are a delight to any family - friendly, affable, charming, anxious to please, well-mannered, the list is endless. To the Leo who feels burning pride in all offspring, they are probably a dream come true. Young Libra has a deep need for company and will probably spend as much time as possible with indulgent Leo. This is flattery indeed for the Lion who loves so much to be needed. The Libran desire to please others and willingness to comply can sometimes develop into an inability to assert themselves when it comes to making decisions. Here Leos can instil a little of their own self-confidence, making the point that you can't please all of the people all of the time. The Libran love of harmony extends to their immediate surroundings and they will respond well to a restful and pleasantly decorated room of their own. Allowing them to use their good taste in these matters can go a long way in developing the

ability to make decisions. Your Leo creativity will be a great inspiration to little Libra and if you can, from time to time, work together on artistic projects so much the better. Librans thrive on good teamwork and you'll be surprised how well your little partner reacts to cooperative ventures, suddenly becoming more assertive, if you hold back your natural instinct to run things. Librans can be good leadership material, rarely as a lone kind of boss giving out orders, but within a group: stimulating and challenging the best out of colleagues can be more effective than being a dictator.

...and now the bad news!

Friction within this parent/child relationship is rare, but Leos are basically life's winners and don't like coming in second place. On the other hand, little Libra sees pushing herself forward as not fair on the others and prefers to stay some-

where in the middle with the rest of the crowd. Any
Leo in this position could be tempted to push their
little one just a little too much, the result being a
lot of resentment and yet a total giving in on the
part of little Libra. This can put a great strain on
the little Balance, whose only wish is to please.
Rows and aggressive arguments are poison to little
Libra, the gentle make up of the Balance just can't
tolerate them. A just and well-reasoned reproach
fits in much better with this youngster's sense of
fairness and don't always expect this little egalitar-
ian to come in top of the class.

♍

THE VIRGO PARENT

The good news!

Little Libra's love of harmony and pleasant surroundings will find comfort in the neat efficiency of the Virgo home. Junior's need of good company and Virgo's fertile mind make for long conversations and a close relationship. Born charmers, little Librans develop early the social graces, and a natural desire to please others can make life easy for the Virgoan parent. This ease, however, though enjoyably undemanding, may not always be in the best interests of the child.

Continually fitting in with the ideas of others may prevent the development of the necessary self-confidence to make a personal decision. The Virgoan parent's ability to sift the facts and draw an accurate conclusion can be of invaluable help in rationalising Junior's dilemma. Encouragement to express opinions – even asking advice on small matters – will slowly build this little diplomat's self-assertion and make difficult decisions easier to resolve. Like Geminis, Virgos are ruled by the communicative planet Mercury, giving them a love

of long conversations and a great pleasure in words almost for their own sake. Your little Libra and you will share this love, and encouragement to talk about and write down daily happenings in a family diary could be a great shared creative outlet for you both. Libran writers abound: even the master of the snappy back-answer, Groucho Marx, was a little Libra. Because other people are so important to the wellbeing of little Libra, he or she will be astonishingly aware of the failings and the foibles of those near to them, giving a great natural ability to make witty and accurate comments on the society around them. This can be hilarious at the age of three or four and later may contribute to a successful career.

...and now the bad news!

You do like things to be just so! Never putting off till tomorrow what you can finish today. Heaven help little Libra who rarely can get around to finishing off whatever project he started trying to make up his mind about an hour ago. Pressure and incessant nagging won't help but will only add to the problem. Pressured Librans, in their desire to please, get even more confused working out what to do for the best. Librans are team workers so better to help them than leave them alone with an awful deadline. Perfection you may seek, but try not to make it beyond Junior's reach and always give him a hand.

The Libra Parent

The good news!

This must be the easiest relationship in the zodiac. Relating to others is so important to this couple that they just can't help getting on. You'd think there couldn't be a snag; well there is but they may just not notice it. Big and little Libra can always see the other person's point of view, get a great kick out of pleasing people and 'fitting in' harmoniously. What's wrong with that? Nothing if one of the partners knows exactly what she or he's going to do. Two Librans, however, each desperately trying to please the other, can debate interminably in a plethora of indecision. The Libran desire for justice demands that every angle is explored before final judgement, but there are times when the need for quick action makes this impossible. This is where Junior needs real help from this intelligent parent. Cutting down the options to manageable proportions, for example 'would you like blue or red?', is less demanding than 'which colour would you like?'. Little points, but they work well in building the confidence of this bright but sometimes too amenable youngster. There should be plenty of opportunity for little Libra to try out the social graces, meeting the many friends that you invite

round to your home. You'll find you have a mini receptionist when it comes to telephone calls too, always getting to the phone first just to see who's calling. Make the most of the telephone now for you'll never get your hands on it from long before this little communicator reaches the teenage years. You know best how to keep another Libran happy. Close companionship, good conversation (from the earliest days, Libran toddlers love to gossip!) and friendly, but never heated, argument, will keep this duet in perfect harmony.

...and now the bad news!

Well only two things really... and you probably won't be very troubled by them. Your shared love of pleasure, luxury and the beautiful things of life could make you both frequent wallowers in extreme and idyllic laziness. Feet up, let's not bother to go out, I'll wash up later. Lovely... where's the bad news? Little Libra will get the habit and may find it difficult to break. Can't be bothered to go to school, fake a headache etc! See what I mean? Set aside special 'lazy times' devoted to shared self-indulgent pleasures and alternate with 'now let's have some fun working together on this little project' spells. You're a Libran... keep the balance! What was the second thing? Just the poor third party in this family, if there is one, having to make all the decisions!

The Scorpio Parent

The good news!

Life is always a grand challenge to you, the powerful Scorpios, and great enthusiasm is thrown into the responsibility of being a parent. Ambitious for your children, you nurture their talents and support and strengthen their weaknesses. Little Librans are charming, sociable, adaptable, and love company. Both parent and child have a strong feeling for artistic pursuits and Scorpio will encourage little Libra's natural good taste and positive talents. The easy-going nature of this youngster will do almost anything to keep their nearest and dearest happy. The dangers in this all too comfortable situation will be obvious to the perceptive Scorpio. In trying to please all of the people all of the time, Junior may not get a look in where personal desires are concerned. Though often content to carry on pleasing, it does little to produce and develop self-confidence. Libran indecisiveness comes from their great sense of balance in all things and in order to reach a judgement everything has to be

taken into consideration. Discussion and debate can do much to familiarise little Libra with the more assertive side of his or her nature. Plenty of visits from young friends will continue the good work. This is where the true Libran talents come in to play and ambitious Scorpio can then see the real worth of this little one, skilfully arbitrating and keeping things running smoothly and amicably even with the most difficult of small colleagues.

...and now the bad news!

Your great strength may read little Libra's less ambitious approach as weakness and without really thinking you could step up the pressure too much for this quite different little being. You just can't turn this sociable 'one of the crowd' into a challenging loner taking on all comers. Don't make the mistake of thinking of little Libra as a loser if she comes tenth or lower in the class. See it as your beneficent offspring, with the greatest sense of fairness in the world, just giving the others a game chance. Seriously though, Libras don't operate on the same wavelength as you. These little wonders are preparing to keep the wheels of life well oiled and running smoothly, holding together all that we value in society. They do this better from the middle rather than up front where they can't see a thing.

THE SAGITTARIUS PARENT

The good news!

Life is always an adventure for you and having a family is just another great enterprise to be thoroughly enjoyed. Sagittarian parents are warm, impulsive, fun-loving friends to their children. No lack of stimulation and excitement in the Archer's household. Little Libra, never a loner, looks for close loving companionship and gets plenty of that with this parent. Rarely sticking to strict routines, the Sagittarian prefers – much to the joy of little Libra – to take each day as a new and exciting project. Whilst giving honest adult answers to all the child's probing questions, loving truth above all things, this parent will support the delightful make-believe necessary in the child's early life. Little Libra's charming manner and desire to please should make for little or no clashes in this good relationship. Though Sagittarius's ideas and enthusiasms will always be amenable to this easy-going youngster, care will have to be taken that little Libra isn't just giving in to keep everything harmonious. These little diplomats are all too happy to lose their entire identity in keeping others'

lives running smoothly. Totally uncomfortable with heated arguments and family rows, this little arbitrator will feel duty-bound to try keeping the peace at all costs. Love has to rule in a household with a Libran in residence. Always trying to be fair to anything and everything, each project will be thought about interminably, weighing the pros and cons in order to come to the fairest conclusion. Often this is carried to extremes on the most trivial matters and Sagittarius will have to step in and point out that once in a while 'just do it and hang the consequences' may be the best answer.

...and now the bad news!

Your love of the truth makes you say exactly what you think, when you think it! Tough on more sensitive mortals and this cookie is one of them where family relationships are concerned. Needing to be loved at all costs, and frequently expecting reassurance, a blunt criticism can inflict damage out of all proportion on little Libra. They really can drive even the most loving parent mad with their indecision! If they think you don't love them Librans will do anything to get back in your good books. Desperate and insecure Librans trying to be everything to everybody just to please are not a pretty sight. Truth is truth but keeping it to yourself more often will make for a better balance.

♑

THE CAPRICORN PARENT

The good news!

With loving care and attention the well-ordered Capricorn home runs smoothly and efficiently. With little to ruffle the young Libran's love of harmony this environment will be ideal. Capricorn parents let their children know just what is expected of them with clearly drawn guidelines for each stage of development. Little Librans, wanting to be close and pleasing to their parents though rarely needing strong discipline or authority, will find great security in knowing where they stand.

These helpful, charming little diplomats will fit in with just about everybody's plans without thought for their own preferences. Fine for family peace but not so hot for developing Junior's individuality. Librans have good logical minds with an unbiased approach that can see all sides of any question; a talent that makes for good arbitrators in later life.

However, a great deal of help and encouragement will be necessary in order to get little Libra to take on the responsibility of a decision. 'Would you like pasta or risotto?' will bring on a pained look and, when he fails to be able to decide, offering another alternative just adds to the confusion. If

you give him a small portion of each on the plate he'll be an age wondering which one to try first! It can drive all but the patient Capricornian to distraction. How lucky little Libra is to have such a long-suffering parent and anyway you do have one of the best-behaved children in your neighbourhood. Not a bad deal! For a Libran artistic choices are the most helpful starters; colours, fabrics, clothes etc., bring out the best of Libran good taste. Keep the options minimal though and you'll win in time.

...and now the bad news!

Patient as you undoubtedly are, there are times when Libra's love of the good life will deteriorate into just plain laziness, not a favourite attribute with you, I'm afraid. Capricorns are notorious for their constant reminders to less conscientious mortals how they should have done such and such a thing, how they could improve themselves if they put their back into it and so on. Lazy as they can sometimes be, and no matter how ineffectual they are in your efficient terms, Librans only want to please their nearest and dearest. Almost all criticism just programs in more indecision and insecurity, so where are you? The true talents of your child will be in the area of human relations and encouragement to work with you will get far better results.

THE AQUARIUS PARENT

The good news!

The Aquarian approach to parenthood is original, unusual, and always interesting for themselves and their children. Plenty of stimulation, a busy social whirl and a constant flux of activity will be a fitting and exciting environment for the companionable little Libran. Good tête-à-tête conversations are the keynote to happiness in this excellent relationship. Little Librans' desire to please, get on, and keep everything running smoothly make them the most charming, amenable and sociable of children. Aquarius's many friends and visitors will be delighted at the manners and confidence displayed by this little diplomat. Libra's good reasoning power makes for steady learning at school though friendships will be of more importance than schoolwork. This need will be easy for Aquarius to understand. However, this youngster's propensity for 'giving in' to keep others happy may need a little watching if it is not to develop into a wishy-washy characteristic. So happy to please,

these little peace-keepers can be oblivious to their own needs and opinions to such an extent that they may lack confidence in making decisions in the future. A difficult one to solve, but encouragement to express judgements in family situations, getting an opinion, acting on it, and praising the results, can be a help. Although loving harmonious relationships, with this parent little Libra will argue more forcefully than is usual. This is not to score points or just to be awkward, but out of sheer love of good debate that is equally enjoyed by the bright-minded Aquarian. You will be able to allow your little Libra the freedom to develop quicker thinking and more ease in taking a stand on the side that logically seems right.

...and now the bad news!

This relationship should rarely deteriorate into real family rows mainly because you both see the other person's side of the question so easily. In some ways this can be to the detriment of little Libra's self-expression. In an atmosphere where each gives in to the other continually, there is little chance to learn what one really wants oneself. If the only motive in life is to please others, individuality can be lost. It's necessary to be quite firm in encouraging the self-will of little Libra, insisting on knowing exactly what he or she would like to be doing from time to time. This will always initially produce evasion as they immediately react by wondering what you would prefer them to say. Don't give a clue, persist and be patient and be delighted when you finally get a true answer!

♓

THE PISCES PARENT

The good news!

Where your children are concerned you can be the biggest softie in the zodiac and it will be hard for you not to go over the top and spoil them with love (much to their delight). Highly intuitive and always just a little bit psychic, Pisces can tune in to the thoughts and feelings of others almost before they have them. Little Libra's need for constant company will find sensitive support with this loving and giving parent. Both parent and child have a natural talent for artistic expression and will share a love of beauty and harmony. This combination of Piscean idealist and Libran diplomat is a certain recipe for everything in the garden being lovely; not a cloud in the sky. Little Librans learn, because of their companionable nature, to understand the other person's point of view. Weighing up the pros and cons, examining every angle, this little one gains a wealth of broad knowledge. However, in order to be absolutely fair in making a decision the process can be slow and painstaking. It would be wise, however, to resist the Piscean

ever-ready, helping hand getting there just a little too soon and too often for young Libra to acquire the confidence to make a judgement. Get Junior to help you with decisions, encourage and admire them when they are made, and the self-reliance will grow. Judgement on colours, house decoration and clothes are less of a problem to this little expert in good taste. Allow complete freedom of choice where this little one's room is concerned; you won't be disappointed at the result. You might even want to ask some advice on your own room. All of this must be accompanied by long, long conversations. Your Piscean sense of fantasy can enrich the thinking of little Libra, broadening his horizons and extending his fast-growing vocabulary.

...and now the bad news!

You may have to make quite a few concessions to a more down-to-earth way of life, certainly in the

early years. Not a great stickler for routine, pre-
ferring to react to situations as and when they
occur, your sometimes chaotic intuitive approach
may cause great confusion to little Libra. Being
continually forced into new reactions before he has
become comfortable with the last way of doing anything can slow down the confidence-building
process. It may seem hard to put a rigid schedule
around such a companionable relationship but the
end result will be beneficial to little Libra and a
delight to you.

ON THE CUSP

Many people whose children are born on the day the sun changes signs are not sure whether they come under one sign or another. Some say one is supposed to be a little bit of each but this is rarely true. Adjoining signs are very different to each other so checking up can make everything clear. The opposite table gives the exact Greenwich Mean Time (GMT) when the sun moves into Libra and when it leaves. Subtract or add the hours indicated below for your nearest big city.

AMSTERDAM	GMT + 01.00	MADRID	GMT + 01.00
ATHENS	GMT + 02.00	MELBOURNE	GMT + 10.00
BOMBAY	GMT + 05.30	MONTREAL	GMT - 05.00
CAIRO	GMT + 02.00	NEW YORK	GMT - 05.00
CALGARY	GMT - 07.00	PARIS	GMT + 01.00
CHICAGO	GMT - 06.00	ROME	GMT + 01.00
DURBAN	GMT + 02.00	S.FRANCISCO	GMT - 08.00
GIBRALTAR	GMT + 01.00	SYDNEY	GMT + 10.00
HOUSTON	GMT - 06.00	TOKYO	GMT + 09.00
LONDON	GMT 00.00	WELLINGTON	GMT + 12.00

DATE	ENTERS LIBRA	GMT	LEAVES LIBRA	GMT
1984	SEP 22	8.33 PM	OCT 23	5.46 AM
1985	SEP 23	2.08 AM	OCT 23	11.22 AM
1986	SEP 23	7.59 AM	OCT 23	5.14 PM
1987	SEP 23	1.45 PM	OCT 23	11.01 PM
1988	SEP 22	7.29 PM	OCT 23	4.45 AM
1989	SEP 23	1.20 AM	OCT 23	10.35 AM
1990	SEP 23	6.56 AM	OCT 23	4.14 PM
1991	SEP 23	12.48 PM	OCT 23	10.05 PM
1992	SEP 22	6.43 PM	OCT 23	3.57 AM
1993	SEP 23	12.23 AM	OCT 23	9.37 AM
1994	SEP 23	6.19 AM	OCT 23	3.36 PM
1995	SEP 23	12.13 PM	OCT 23	9.32 PM
1996	SEP 22	6.00 PM	OCT 23	3.19 AM
1997	SEP 22	11.56 PM	OCT 23	9.15 AM
1998	SEP 23	5.37 AM	OCT 23	2.59 PM
1999	SEP 23	11.32 AM	OCT 23	8.53 PM
2000	SEP 22	5.28 PM	OCT 23	2.48 AM
2001	SEP 22	11.05 PM	OCT 23	8.26 AM
2002	SEP 23	4.56 AM	OCT 23	2.18 PM
2003	SEP 23	10.47 AM	OCT 23	8.09 PM
2004	SEP 22	4.31 PM	OCT 23	1.50 AM

John Astrop is an astrologer and author, has written and illustrated over two hundred books for children, is a little Scorpio married to a little Cancerian artist, has one little Capricorn psychologist, one little Pisces songwriter, one little Virgo traveller and a little Aries rock guitarist. The cats are little Sagittarians.